Corvus Witch

A Poetic Corpus

ISBN 978-0-578-64167-6

Cover Art Stefan Keller

Dedication

To Nicole Joslyn and Alan Lowrie.

Jessica – For putting up with my nonsense.

Paul the Cat – For creating above said nonsense with me.

Keeley, Mom, Dad, Jessica, Shaun, Brayden, Aubrie, Jennifer, Josh, Preston, Landon, Gail, the Ligon and Baker families

Special Thanks to: Steve Ruff, Damon Shields, John Bushey, Dorson Foster, Mark Lyons.

Introduction

Corvus Witch is separated into three chapters with five different feeling and ideals:

~ *Within* – The darkness of pain. Poems that are not sugar coated, they are the bare naked truth of the internal struggle and sadness that only we can know, alone in our darkest hour, when we feel so very far away from everything. "Her" and "She" are a central theme in many of my poems. Almost all are real with infinite sadness, hopes for the future or innocent happiness. I have lost touch with all of them but their memory is here within the pages. Final ideal for *Within*, the historic struggle and the never ending fight to push away evil thoughts

~ *And Yet You Continue To Provoke The Night* –
Poems dedicated to Nicole Joslyn and Alan
Lowrie.

~ *Daily Grind* – Retired pastor Frank Moore, has
written one poem a day for the last 50 years. I
decided to give it a try, to see how long I could
go without missing a day.

Within

Ode To The Romantic Within

An unloved lover in a dreamer's dream.
Prince Charming within unheroic minds.
Liquid souls dance upon a moonbeam,
Try contemplating this for all lost time.

Breathtaking rhymes flowing in conjunction,
Means nothing to the unfelt compassion.
How can words stand primordial function,
If they cannot comply their vogued fashion.

The constant beauty found within my head,
Falls stone cold to my hideous outside.
Constant commotion of pain almost dead,
Within my own reality I hide.

I and Cyrano are long lost brothers,
We are the real outcasts of true lovers.

Has Anyone Seen My Valentine

A table with empty chairs
For him a long forgotten memory.
Now dark and endlessly vacant
Was the place where she sat,
As moonlight danced upon
every strand of hair.

Has anyone seen my Valentine?

The candles have since burned away.
He takes position once again at the
head of the table.
A past emotional flood returns to
A happier day.
Holding back tears he whispers,

Has anyone seen my Valentine?

She was a princess locked in heart
He the prince with his soul the key
Once the two combined...
Their bond was never to grow apart.
Now she was gone, his candle of passion
burned out that very day,

Has anyone seen my Valentine?

Down the hall into a bedroom
Of shattered hope.
Implanted in the mattress an
Indentation of her slender frame
Calls out, "I am always near."
But still it was hard to cope
With the fact that his companion
Was no longer here.

Has anyone seen my Valentine?

Onto the porch, where he proposed
To her his heart, overlooking a
Sea of peace and tranquility.
A promise now replaced by an ocean
Of questions and a typhoon of hostility.

Has anyone seen my Valentine?

Snow White bit off too much of the
Apple this time and Prince Charming
Sealed his own fate with a kiss.
Her every waking moment was more
Beautiful then where the angels tread...
A dream he would always miss.

Has anyone seen my Valentine?

An empty table surrounded by
Empty chairs and the ghost of a breeze
Where a happy future was once planned
Now but the wisp of a memory drifting
Through the trees.
A candle snuffed too early in time

Has anyone seen my...?

A Walk in Time

Silent on the eve of
Carpe Diem.
Wandering a course of
Lightening and sunshine kisses.
To cry through someone else's
eyes, if only for a second to
relieve her heavy laden heart.

The spider of passion creates
a webbed cloud of despair
heavy on her soul - the silver
lining poisoned by venom.

Yet she wanders a course of
lightening and sunshine kisses.
A demure concourse of solemnness
and despair create an emergence
of bitter memories,

Constant on - Steadfast on - Never on - Or Death?

Femme The Beast

She treads on somber thru,
my head.
Reliving the litigation of a past,
almost dead.
Candid banter stark,
in review.
She turns as a two toned
leaf anew.
Could still this be a fortnight,
of forgotten time.
Or return to the head drunk,
on a symposium of angels and wine.
A tranquil symphony of peace calls to the winds,
songs through the trees.
And still there lingers
a Nordic battle cry upon every gentle breeze.
She stoops to conquer an underlying heart,
stopping only to retrieve each and every
shattered part.
What winds the winding road,
to the soul of unhappiness?
In direction this restitute,
is what she'll always miss.

Dance

She colored me blind
dancing mutely
to a blue green symphony.

Among waves of grain
and snow capped
mountain backdrops.

She dances free
between the sill and the shade
with the stars of night.

Toe to Toe
Cheek to Cheek
Heart to Heart

And nothing shall
come between them
until the dawn.

Her Choice

Blind to truth
Deceived by memories
Bruised and scorned
In the end.

She falls into an abyss
Of mistakes and idolatry.

Once she stood by Him
Now false understatements
Rule the world she once believed in.

Truth to be sought...
But answers never come
To those who understand
The understood.

On a fence...
To one the straight
To the other the crooked.

Sodom or Calvary?

Into consciousness
Fall or stand is the
Question in her heart.

Fall for now and
Forever she will not
See the light or love.

The Great Butterfly Chaser

Running thru a field of daises
In her favorite overall's
and Wonder Woman tee-shirt.

So proud she dressed herself
This morning before
Playing in the dirt.

The Great Butterfly Chaser

Barefoot on the grass
In a child's fantasy
Fishing net in hand.

Free as the Mourning Dove
My little green eyed princess
in a summer wonderland.

She Chases After Butterflies

Drifting away on a cloud
The subtle morning breeze
playing in her hair.

Where sweet innocence
And angels play
without a care.

The Great Butterfly Chaser

With mischievous eyes
Net poised above her head
She seeks out her opponent.

Alas...

The butterfly takes wing
in a display
of green eloquence.

She Chases After Butterflies

The game again is on
Both floating off the ground.
Her little butterfly soul
Almost Heaven Bound.

Dark Mind Trap

Into my dark mind trap
Set up against a pure white
back drop.

In a world of, *What's on tap?*
A near still life under a surreal
big top.

To be known for what once was, now
balancing on a tight-wire of what wants
to be.

Heavy in life, to change somehow
My urges fade and my dark mind trap
Is all I see.

Daises and roses surround my fatal soul
A never quenched love exhumes my poisoned
heart.

To be solitaire in life, an unobtainable whole.
I pull understanding petal from petal
apart.

Once again to drop in the pond
To change around and come in oneness
fast.

To decompose a time of fair and fond.
Returning to a memory future of a
dark mind trap past.

"rAiN"

Red As INsult,

Working AgainsT thE caveRns,

oF Long fOrgOtten Demise,

 and trite SEAS of carnage.

Red As INsult

Down the spiRals Of turbulent WiNds

          anD back up InsidE again

trying to escape her raging STORM

                    only
                     in
                    time
                     to
                    learn

we'D all be bEtter off deAD, before the rain.

The Long Awaited Arrival

A hush befell the trees
When I spotted the overwhelming
Beauty.

A fawn within a long forgotten
Jungle.

When last I fell upon such a
Lovely creature I was young and foolish.

And with harsh words and quick motions
I chased her away.

Solemnly I lay upon the deep, plush
Autumn floor and let stone and moss surround
My hated heart.

Never again did I move, laying there
Watching the fawns go past... never stopping.

Lonely in the night, me being my
Only companion. My soul dying with the
Winter and waiting to be reborn again.

This fawn stopped on a
New spring morning,
Reminding me of who I am.

This one does not pass the mossen rock
But cracks it with her stare.

She dare not get any closer though
But just looks.

Within her beautiful eyes I
Once again see that I am
Not lost but alive.

All That Matters

Her heart a precious golden
Lock.
My love the diamond
Key.

She is the jewel that adorns my
Day.
I the thief who steals her in the
Night.

A rose in the coldest
Snow.

Donna Julia of my very – But meager
Existence.
Alas I am the Phantom rather than
Don Juan.

The thorn in the dove that is
Her.
To me her love is all that
Matters.

What the heck is he talking about?

Decadence of a once dead man,
Returning as a star struck soul.
Soaring on the wings of an eagles mind,
Some wondering of an apathy whole.

A wandering heart east of the sun,
A restless spirit west of the moon.
Trinitized under broken glass,
Crucified at the still of noon.

Pondering lore still in creation,
Fulfilling a loss still in the making.
Standing tall in the shadow of doubt,
A love I am obviously faking.

Into a realm of conflict and anarchy,
Must on and up the beaten path.
In life I am the prisoner,
My memory releasing the burden of wrath.

To care as someone else's peace,
Unloved as only I can.
Subtle to the crying heart,
A glitch in the master plan.

And still I part my hair,
As if the ever changing tide.
I tripped on my own soul,
We run but cannot hide.

To the Lady

Golden hair or immortal halo?
Great blue eyes unmatched by the sea.
Beauty comparable to an angel
A femme created by fantasy.
Innocent as the dawn,
Witty as the day,
Trusting as a fawn
In night's fallow shades of grey.
Adam's true life Eve,
God's answer to a prayer.
I still wonder in disbelief
Is it a halo or golden hair?

Muoia dalla nostra mano

Walking thru your Babylon,
STONED and persecuted.
They call to you on the street,
every time you close your eyes.
Beckoning you home.

You belong with us.

A fog of anger and agony,
clouds your subconscious.
Pain your only begotten friend,
peace and happiness once,
now only a glimpse.

Join us my child.

Into a world of euphoric color,
and oscuro sesso.
Mistake your master,
still you blindly light
your peace maker.

Our world is yours.

Drifting on a plateau,
of numbness,
and impellent obsession.
Until you're reduced to nothing,
e siete niente.

Muoia dalla nostra mano.

Valor of Conscience

Pariahs of insanity
Harbingers of discontent
Gasp out in callous winds –

Fare thee well love
Fare thee well hope
Fare the well to remorse

On their scrangled pipes
of maliced vanity
And Lucifer before the dawn

Skaal to the stillborne afterlife
Outside the tempest moon
Still she wounds me phantomwise.

ThErApY?

Desolate stones on a turnpike
watercolors washed away.
With crimson blue insanity
as a solitary color in my mind.

Whom is it we truly pay?
To soon we seek so shallow we find...

Paradox Progress...

I grasp upon the sling blade
in one hand
And caress a daisy
in the other.

Wandering my souls decadent land
Searching for a catalyst brother.

As pestilence grips
with bone white knuckles.
Hearts begin to create
a mind of their own.

Loves straight jacket tighten their buckles
and the center does not hold for the unknown.

Witness

Above incandescent
black clouds
Electric storms
thunder across the mind.

As a false witness stands
in ignorant crowds
Giving solutions to answers
we cannot find.

Prophetically
adolescent
counter phrasing
to paralyze the norm.

Lighting the torch
and ablaze the stage
Where lunatic
puppets perform

Self-righteous dances
with backwards knowledge
to stand and hold
their funeral pyre.

Away from God
and long ago hope
They burn away
in lakes of fire.

We Marionettes

From heart to head
to soul, the marionette
travels by trap doors.

Strings cut and retied
each second we love
and every moment we war.

He has you wrapped around
his finger as the
goldest wedding band.

Who controls who
master of mind or
master of pleasure?

We stand united falling
from the stage of truth and light...

...into a safety net
of lust and
despair.

Monsieur Baal-zebub
the puppeteer
forms the question:

When is it we cut
the strings and reattach
them above all else?

Death Search of an Ancient Viking

The twisted sea
Two souls apart,
Whispers a plea
Within my heart.

Forever far
As I may roam,
A silver star
Shall guide me home.

My lady fair
I laid to rest,
In mind I bare
Her family crest:

RESPECT IS ALL
YOU GIVE AWAY,
NO HEART SO SMALL
WILL SEIZE THE DAY.

Her sweet revenge
Some burning need,
I shall avenge
Her fertile seed.

A dying rose
Within my hand,
Two lives disposed
On foreign land.

For several years
Of hide and seek,
They slither in fear
For slaying the meek.

NOW...

A broken man
With heart that's frail,
No course or plan
I did set sail.

To find her star
On a vast sea,
Will heal my scar
Called eternity.

Naked Remnants

She stands backwards in
Powdered sugar snow.
A world of confused peace
orbits her bitter soul...

...Naked...

... she clutches near the
waking dream of love.
Still, it melts as
blueberry icicles...

...Remnants...

... pouring from her bloodless
lips red as wine,
To struggle no more
with her dark monster...

...Hope...

...She draws across the
once, so happy blade.
To pour salt in and pain...

...Now...

...her little angelic soul
almost heaven bound and
happy.

DOWN THE LANE

MOTHER LUCIFER'S GONE
DOWN THE SHADY LANE
A GUN IN HER HAND AND
A SOUL LOST IN ETERNITY.

DRIFTING ON A SEA OF CONFUSION
GETTING MORE AND MORE
LOST IN EVERYTHING.
THE WORLD BETRAYED HER
REVENGE IS A SWEETLY UNDYING
OBSESSION THAT ONLY SHE CAN FEEL.

SHE IS COLD TO A WORLD
THAT DOES NOT EXIST
FOR ONLY SHE EXISTS
IN A WORLD THAT IS COLD
GOD HAS FORSAKEN ME FOR I HAVE FORSAKEN
MYSELF.

THE GUN AND PULL THE TRIGGER.

Wastari

The hour has come,
Rats at the cross
And burden in our
Heart.

A nation on the rise,
Hope on the decline
At the center...

Paradox Progress

A past look at our
Present future
Reveals all that
Cannot be and
All that is.

Dark is our
Bright future
Because we forgot...

...Christ.

Alone

A new dawn breaks
with the lone call
of a rooster,
Each morning I face
The mirror,
It reflects the
roosters call...

Alone...

Hiding each true
emotion
With a smile...
"Nothing's wrong,"
Christ shared
My burden....
To have so many
and in the end no one...

Alone...

Who with the heart
is remembered
when there is...
The look.

"The outside is a shell,
it is what is on the inside..."
My "friends" all say
but they – like the rest
of this shallow society
remember the outside...

Alone...

They are cardboard
cutouts...
All of them.
I am real;
three dimensional...

Alone...

When the winds
of change
come about – they
will be blown away;
and I will be left standing...

Alone.

Into the Dark

Alone I walk the beach,
into the dark of night.
Retracing the steps,
of life in the light.

As the darkness,
leads me into sin.
I wait for his arms,
to take me in.

"I am unloved,"
I begin to cry.
Then I remember,
"for me He sent His son to die."

His love and I,
are not that far apart.
He waits for
me in my heart.

All I have to do is
walk into His light.
And out of the
Darkness of my night.

My First Poem

As I lay next to you on the sands of time,
all is quite except for the distant sound
of the church bells chime.
Each chime seems to tell us that
love is like a doorway between fantasy and
reality, and though you wish you could
stay there in that doorway forever and just
forget all of life's troubles and endeavor, you can
not, for just as the bells chime ends so do
the signs of love that one person sends to the
other. After the signs die if those bells of love
should ever happen to chime again it would be a
sin for you shall be with another and I
Shall be without a lover.

*Written when I was only 16, it is bad, but how many poets
actually share their first writing?*

Until

Until the stars
cease to dot the sky
until the ocean
currents all run dry
until God becomes
"just some guy"
and until the very
day I die

I WILL LOVE U.

Another Sleepless Night

Another sleepless night
It's getting late and
I am feeling
kind of seasick.

Ease my mind
with a photograph
of Romeo and Juliet
up the garden path

and I wish I could be
there with her.

The Charred Remains Of A Burning Question

I dreamed of love
Long before the day doth glow.
Only to crash and burn
Among the stars,
In your eyes.

Nothing so cold
Or far away.
Reaching out for
a known answer --
"Where did it stray?"

"From the conception."
Came a whisper to a cry.

In a blue funk, filled with
Lust emaciated love,
guilt hits like emerald
bullets through the
hearts soulless window.

Abandoned in a desperate
torrent of tears -- I give up
on hope and drown
alone in decadence...

...all the while

a picture cascades
through my mind --
pained in hues
of remorse and
toned with apathy --

of Lolita cloaked
in innocence and
immersed in a
celestial glow.

Cavalcading with a rose
clenched tightly to her
breast and a thorn
out stretched within
reach of my hand.

Queried, pondering the
distortion in my mind.
Death comes a light
through the haze.

I'm getting closer

Grasping the slipknot
in my frail hand
and waiting for reality
to lose its edge.

You can't comprehend this fear...

"Where did it stray?"

"From the conception."
Came a whisper to a cry.

She Took Me On

She took me on
and I became the
worst version of myself.

Now in the mirror of
shattered dreams stands
half a man I thought
no one could break.

Time killed the messenger
on his chariot of fire.
I should have known,
To late she's gone.

Remorse came faunching
like a banshee for a brief
moment then copacetic sets in.

Seeing Jones (light quanta)

Hop in the car
and drive,
Just to hear
Myself talk.

Does no good
just like speaking
to a brick wall
I careen into....

Glass and mortar,
raining down
flooding the
river I become

Caught in the
undertow
floating
amongst the
shadows

Dissipate at
dawn with
the sun in my
eyes........

I hop in the car
and drive,
just to hear
myself talk.

Every beginning has to end

You are my every word
Floating down the cliff
Into an abyss of pestilence.

You're getting tired of your skin
Shedding the new
Into lightning catacombs.

Uneasy in my electric chair
I begin to swell and become
An island unto myself.

Segregated from the callous
Wind that stings my heart
And sways judgment.

Our circle has no center
To hold firm the travesty
Of a shattered fairy tale.

Ever Down

Ever Down
bleeding on
the inside.

Hop on the
bandwagon
for a nostalgic
free will ride.

Head to head
tooth and nail
feeding on the
meek – consuming
the frail.

Break neck speeds
end in conformity
of zero tolerance
and a dry spell of
copacetic abstinence.

Groovy Poem in D Minor

All I know
is that I am.
I cannot grow
if I am damned.

An April death
in June weather.
There is nothing left
of December.

I once believed
that's why I drown.
Some small reprieve
from going down.

Reality's fake
I feel no sorrow.
A big mistake
For tomorrow.

Winter Daises

She gave me winter daises
in the middle of Spring
standing before me
upon angels wings
she said she'd love me
unconditionally.
Thru my soul lost window
words I cannot believe.
I turned my eyes from her
and prayed to the Son
He said you'll love her
Forever plus one.

...And Yet You Continue To Provoke The Night

Nicole

Send the angels of remorse
A life ended too soon.
I never knew her but she was beautiful.

I wish I could have done something
If something could have been done
To be there, to be strong, to stand up.

She did not need to die in the dark alone
I would have held her hand and smiled softly
Innocently, she knows the way to Heaven.

Alan

God places special angels on this earth
Most of us do not notice them until it is too late.

For those who were touched by the special angels,
They can never forget.

Alan walked among us unique,
Everyone knew he was a special angel.

He continues his work now,
In Heaven as he did on earth.

I

Who will procure the heart?
Everlasting happiness
Or the decay of time?

We never foresee the
Trials just around the bend
Will we continue tomorrow
Or cease today?

The mind does not fathom
Contemplating this daily
Until the final moment arises
And we are left with that only.

II

What low this bitter hatred is?
No one has wronged you
Yet you feel the need to kill
The innocence of radiant light
With your enveloping darkness.

III

Doomed to repeat
The past
We do not need
To drag
Its violent memory into
The future.

IV

And yet
You continue to
Provoke the night.

Daily Grind

I

Still on, Still on
The beaten path
Thus fate I feel
Thy bloodlust wrath
I'm gone, I'm gone
Until the 'morrow
To sow the seeds
Of merciless sorrow.

II

Burn the eternal fire...
Burn the internal fire...
Which one toils and
Which one will collect
The victorious spoils.

III

One gives to the day
All that they can
Believe in every second
That you are doing good
And leave me wholly
To the night.

IV

Souls apart and
So thin the veil
Save for now
Our coffin nail.

Deus Vult

Love reverts back to a whole
Through space and day
Over the mired beyond.

Time reverts back to a goal
Abysmal grey
A silence for which we are fond.

Life reverts back to a dream
My thought and hope
For an undeserved second chance.

Infinity moves forward to redeem
The power to cope
Within the world without a glance.

V

Her aura floats away,
A ghost on the morning mist
Wrapping me tightly
In the sea breeze
And drowning
My wasted being.

VI

This uncanny dwelling
Holds a dreamscape
Backed off from reality.
The clock stands still
Yet my heart moves on.
A cautious memorial to the past.

VII

The path of life
Is beaten by lessons
Some steps are back
Some veer off
But in the end
All return to the
Heart of the matter.

VIII

I still realize my love for you
At this very moment,
Standing on this very second,
Wrapped in this insignificantly
Quantifiable amount of time.

The overwhelming nature
Of it begs for more
But I will take what you
Can produce on a daily basis
And know it is your all.

IX

I have blown away
The Stately rise to nothing.

Seen the World decay
And Nation crumble.

Been broken in spirit
And made whole in body.

I search for you now,
A harbinger of design.

I know you are out there
Though I've never seen you.

How many more onyx bullets
Can I endure without giving up?

How many more vacant eyes
Must I fall into until you're there?

X

Shad, Mesh and Abe
Like a moth upon the flame
Doth we all go too
Or fall alight in shame.

XI

East of the sun
Betrothed
West of the moon
And they were
More than contented
Until that ill-fated eclipse in June.

XII

I saw her on the sea shore
Desolate and stark against
The setting backdrop.

Still rays emanated from
Her aurora making the
Sun mute and drab,
The water colorless
And the sky opaque.

I wondered if she could feel
My soul from this distance
But my heart was empty
And my being transparent.

She was the purest snow white angel
And I was a bargaining chip for hell.

XIII

Breathe slowly
The breath of
Her perfume
So natural and
Wonderful in
Simplicity
I'd give everything
To smell her
Intoxication now.

XIV

What then of life,
Steal the heart
Or steel the head?
Where does the soul lie
In autumn colored embers?

XV

Stealth from Blackout
Across the lightening sea.
Bandy about and nary a doubt
I long to consume, her electricity.

XVI

Crash the lightening
Against my waves
Thunder rolls
From deep within.

I long to know your
Tumultuous skies.
What downpours despair
And low pressures force
Gales upon my reaching sun.

Again I struggle to break the
Wall of fog you have built
And fortified around your
Radiant solar being.

XVII

I have seen hate and love
In the same burning ember.

Experienced life pouring
From the intricate dance of flames.

Seared knowledge in
Translucent carnal fires.

None compare to the burning
Passion I see in her eyes.

XVIII

Reality fades and the imaginary
Take flight in the gloaming.

Scarlet haze through a burnt fire
What fear and loathing exists in this
The end of day.

The living retire and the nocturnal
Rise for the lonesome night.

XIX

Can you believe I am
Standing here silhouetted
Against your beauty?
I fear this is but a dream.
A beautifully horrible
Waking dream.

XX

Imaginary landscapes
Broad brush strokes
Of delusional tranquility.
Up and down the mauve
Colored carpet
Uninspired art work
Feels nice but looks
Like a train wreck.

Never Touch It

Lost in my own self worth
Trailing in the eyes of the observer
I cannot feel my being through
The distant ghost of your heart.

Wrapped awkwardly in the
Recycled tears of the martyr...
Clouds once of security
Now deny me slumber
Drained and colorless I fall.

Life comes soon enough to heaven.
The clear, blue sky... never touch it.

Renewed Appreciation

I wondered if you'd find me
Here beside myself.
Not because I was lonely
(By any stretch of virile imagination).
No, I was merely hoping to catch a glimpse
Of your beauty through fresh eyes.

New Loving Of Day

I wake up every morning
Already falling out of love with the day.
Then I roll over and see you sleeping
And I realize what the sun rises true worth is.

Have You Ever Lived In A Shadow?

Have you ever lived in a shadow?
Dark, foreboding and desperate.
The cold of its night lasts forever
Until the gloaming true.

Only in the still of twilight does the
Shadow walk with everyone.
And everyone walks in the shadow
I need to dwell there too.

Have you ever lived in a shadow?
Dark, foreboding and desperate.
A void across the counter cultures of time
Infinite in thy gloom.

Give up your darkness increasing
Lose the length of day.
A covenant of ominous desire
Our closest companion of truth.

Have you ever lived in a shadow?
Dark, foreboding and desperate.
A stoic penchant before the dawn
And Lucifer after the day doth set.

Quasi human in steadfast nature
Oh, serenely melancholy one
Perpetuated by a dream
Caught up in a sallow shade.

Have you ever lived in a shadow?
The dark, foreboding, desperate forevermore.

In The End

All the words swim together,
As the confession of a man reflects
The destination behind the mask.

Drenched convictions
Somewhere in the dawn.
Silhouetted tears and
Chaos defined lines
Discard dreams to dust.

Temporal carriages take him too far,
Through a fog of useless time and
Internal self slumber behind the
Translucent veil.

I, Fog

Looming over the factories
A gloomy fog not of nature.
An acidic appreciation for
My distraught intuition.

I float through the city
Wandering the air alone.
Vapid apathy, my cold chill
Condensed old soul blinding.

Where can I roll along
Free of my torturous past?
I am impending doom
One should leave me be.

Again, Forever

Again, forever I dance
Away love.
Give away hope.
Share precious moments.
In the end I seem to
Procure loneliness,
Drawn in darkness,
Sting from sadness.

TBTN

I fear the violence of this world
Violence of the word,
Violence of the hand.

One voice joining millions
NOW, to overpower.

Corvus Witch

Corvus witch of idle fire,
Striking song for demon choir.
Raven-esque and Renaissance in form,
She treads alight the magnetic storm.
Eyes incandesce in an opulent stare,
She coaxes with a come-hither aire.
Ending with her athame to the head,
To sweet the relief when you're already dead.

Serpentine

Dulcimers droning in time to space
Abuse hidden under a pancake face.
She primps and preens a gauntlet of desire
Inside the rage of an ashen fire.
He sleeps, she stands knife in hand
And she hopes that God will understand.

Winter's Fire

A casual fire burns in a room where hope
Once dwelled and love went bubbling over.

The smell of buttercups and daisies replaced
By the rank dankness of musty mold.

Like clockwork a happy prayer was said
Before the joyous retired for the evening.

Now he sits, withering away alone in his solidarity
Was there ever a smile that glanced
Across his leathery mouth?

What happened to the family that spent
Their overflowing glee on each other?

Only the earthen cellar floor knows for sure.

June 1832

Poet,
Transient,
Or Laureate
Rise up, Rise up
I say.

Barnstormers,
Brainstormers
And Non Conformers
Rise up, rise up
Against the day.

Republicans,
Insurgents
And Malcontents
The National Guard
Is close at hand
Rise up, Rise up
For your freedom and
Take a bitter stand.

Vanity's Ball

Hell's winter of discontent,
Falls upon me lo these many days.
I gambled with loves frailty
And lost, breaking heart.

Absconded, forlorn and pitiful
You pray your righteous tears
Will cleanse my black jade soul.

I am not so forthright
With the solution
To your aging queries
About the dwelling of
Passion inside the
Poisoned being.

Here is a jovial befuddlement
To while away the mass of time:

Is the earth, sun or my sinful nature
The center of the universe proper?

Unkind of Karma

Unkind of Karma
Lead me to her

Unkind of Karma
Lead her to me

Unkind of Karma
Dissolve into destiny

Before you DESTROY another life
Before YOU destroy another life

Unkind of Karma
Lead me to her

Unkind of Karma
Lead her to me

Unkind of Karma
Dissolve into destiny

Dinner In Hell

Oblique Obelisk
Mounted steadfast in my mind.
Where evil, the devil,
And my old soul dines.
Who says I cannot smell the brimstone?
It is all that surrounds and consumes me.
Who then...who then...who then
Will understand my insanity?

Past Pondering

I wonder what lies behind the veil.
Is it the classic unraveling of time?

I ponder what lies beyond the door.
Could it be your laminated soul?

What lies beyond the shaded window?
An inhabitable life undeserved.

I steeled against what is beyond the heart.
A nurturing nature beyond the tarnish.

Lost

I walk your waste land
Dark and depressing.
Unicorns and rainbows lay waste
In desperate isolation.

You are not to blame
Provocation did not
Come from within
Your radiant solar being.

He stood with blackest heart
Uncaring to your passion.
You must depart in haste
Before your expiration.

Short

Struggling metaphoric
A temporary division of time
Waxing lament of the exotic
Awash by the tide.

Plutonic Splendor

Entangled in her gravity
Wrapped in your envy
I try to pull away.

Complacent in space
And disillusioned
by the chase
I try to start fresh
Each day.

I close my eyes
Inhaling the memory
Of your Spiritual bouquet.

Archaic Room

In my 4x7 archaic room
The rancidity of decay sickens
Even the strongest man.

In my 4x7 archaic room
Dwells the rotting stench
of earthen musk.

In my 4x7 archaic room
Rats gnaw on fleshy bone
Through casket holes.

In my 4x7 archaic room
If only they knew
I was still alive.

Autumn Revenge

Questioning the country road
Fast wind, carving space.
Trees leaves pyre in splendorous grace
Now thieving time for winter's tomorrow.

The Love Of A Stranger

What can I say?
What can I do?
How can I stay?
If I don't know you.
What should I say?
Why should I care?
Words cannot convey,
How I feel in your despair.

What Wrongs May Befall

An incendiary life void of the chase,
A wet blanket still in my case.
A tweak of fate one way or the other,
And they all fall one after another.
Which decision is the one that's right?
I'll find out one darkened night,
The pitch is black, devil by my side.
I will take whatever may come in stride.

The Other

I think about her everyday
The true terror felt
I cannot convey.
I gaze around a broken man
An insatiable burning
I don't understand.

Bring 'Em Back

Good night stars and best of luck.
May you stay strong and proper
Through the night and guide
Our boys home without yield.

They never gave up on us
May you never give up on them
Oh, little stars above
Bring the troops back
With nary a waiver.

Dwell Timer

Could I spin around
The sin dwellers head?

Will I know a time when
The urban dwellers dead?

Would I fall for the
Romance dwellers ways?

All are perpetuated
In melancholy days.

Another Meeting

Silent light
Surrounds the room.
There is no one here
To feel my gloom.
One more meeting
Inside this place.
One more time
Faking a happy face.

End Of 'Morrow

Born to exist outside the realm
Cautioning winds and killer apathy
Slay autumn in blind haste.
Time still hinders immortality
Beside Venus as she bleeds and
Poseidon weeps for eternity.

Spirit Through A Hazy Memory

Spirit through a hazy memory,
Why do you stalk me like thine enemy?
I have always been so good to you.
Stood up steadfast, strong and true.
Spirit through a hazy memory,
Why do you stalk me like thine enemy?
Is it because you ingested sugar of lead?
Or because all that remains of you
Is deaths head?

How

How far have you cried?
How many times have your
Feelings been set aside?
How many times has your soul
Been awash by the tide?
How many times have you
Been dead on the inside?

Forget Me In Death

Obtusely irrelevant
Is my life so mundane.

I say a short prayer to
Dull the constant pain.

Re-writing our history
So you wouldn't miss me.

Below, below, below

Quiet please as I
Stay down below.

Long Since Disarming

Can one create a gentle breeze,
With a gallant smile of
Long ago lore?

Could a knight slay a dragon,
With a simple look
And no gore?

Could I betroth someone,
I do not know and be
Happy forever more?

Stand The Earth Still (my final poem)

Willows sway in time
To a tune defined
By the wind.

Grassy maracas
Played by bare feet
And our rolling bodies.

Stand the earth still
So I can lie awake in the
Field and take my time

Exploring the curvaceous
Resolution of your body.

About the Author

Magician, escape artist, movie producer, poet.

Shawn Ness has accomplished things few would dream about and most would never contemplate.

This is the corpus of his poetic endeavor - good, bad and ugly. Corvus Witch: A Poetic Corpus features the works of the author under pen names: Sky Larson, JT Sky & Sean Padoric Peterson. Covering the years 1992-2010.

The author lives in Fond du Lac, Wisconsin with his wife, daughter and a cat named Paul.

One Week Challenge

Sunday: Write a poem

Monday: Do something good for someone else without the expectation of praise.

Tuesday: Write a poem

Wednesday: Alter a person's life for the better without telling people.

Thursday: Write a poem

Friday: Bring a little joy without posting to social media about it.

Saturday: Eat copious amounts of bacon.

Let's make the world a little better place.